For my folks and siblings, and the exceptional people at Nobrow that helped make this book.

But not for those who talk loudly in the theater.

An Illustrated History of Filmmaking © Nobrow 2018.

This is a first edition published in 2018 by Nobrow Ltd.
27 Westgate Street, London E8 3RL.

Text and illustrations © Adam Allsuch Boardman 2018.

Adam Allsuch Boardman has asserted his right under the Copyright, Designs and Patents Act, 1988, to be identified as the Author and Illustrator of this Work.

Published in the US by Nobrow (US) Inc.

Printed in Latvia on FSC® certified paper.

ISBN: 978-1-910620-40-3
Order from www.nobrow.net

ADAM ALLSUCH BOARDMAN

AN ILLUSTRATED HISTORY OF FILMMAKING

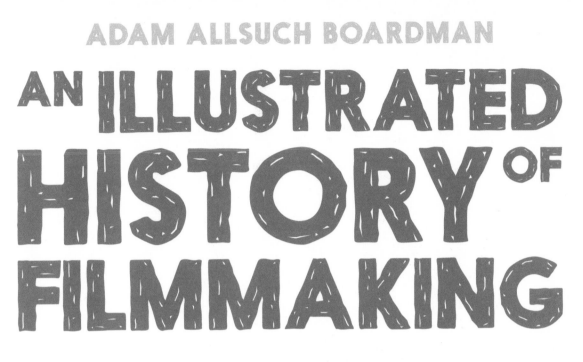

NOBROW

LONDON | NEW YORK

CONTENTS

INTRODUCTION

Most of us have some memory of the first time we went to the movies. In my case, it was the special edition re-release of *The Empire Strikes Back* (1997), and as it was my birthday I was allowed into the projection room. Seeing those huge projectors that made motion pictures possible was an incredible experience. Since that moment, I have been fascinated with filmmaking equipment and how it all works.

With this book I will do my best to explore some of the devices, methods and people that have shaped filmmaking through history, from aspirational foundations to commercial empires. You may notice that I don't discuss the history of animation, as I really think that is deserving of its own book and not just a tacked-on chapter or two. It's my hope that you'll be intrigued enough by this book to go and make your own forays into this fascinating field.

PREHISTORY

PLAYING WITH LIGHT

Moving images are a surprisingly ancient form of entertainment. Interacting with light can be traced to the prehistoric discovery of fire, but it was in ancient East Asia that light was first used to show narrative scenes.

A Bronze Age person enjoying the splendid light and warmth of fire.

Oil lamps were often ornately decorated.

In these shadow plays, puppets were held between a screen and a light source to create the shadows of characters. To this day, there is still a tradition of shadow play in Indonesia, Thailand and Malaysia.

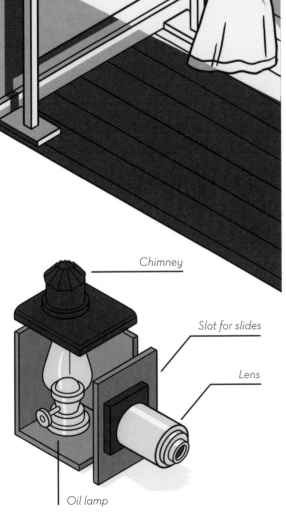

Magic lanterns were commonly used by academics. Here I've imagined Ada Lovelace using one to demonstrate her work on the Difference Engine.

Chimney

Slot for slides

Lens

Oil lamp

Old Devices

The optical phenomenon of the camera obscura is likely just as ancient. When the sun shone through holes in animal hides or caves, our ancestors may have discovered that this produced an inverted projection. During the 17th century, there was a fresh interest in optics that led to the invention of the telescope and microscope, and in 1659 Dutch mathematician and astronomer Christiaan Huygens created a working "magic lantern", what we now might call a projector.

CHRISTIAAN
HUYGENS

This device involved a lens, a light source and a painted glass slide. Lanterns could be used as tools for teaching and storytelling, and the operators could quickly change slides to create the illusion of movement.

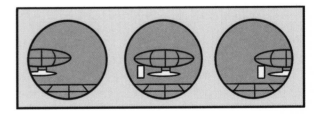

A slide depicting a floating airship.

19TH CENTURY

THE 1800s

The Industrial Revolution ushered in a great era of scientific discovery. Trailblazing explorers and tyrannical empires connected the world, allowing information and technology to be shared more quickly than ever.

ZOETROPE

Among the new devices created at this time was the Zoetrope, a revolving drum with a sequence of images on the inside. When the drum is spun at high speed, the brain processes the images as continuous movement.

Film

The word 'film' refers to capturing images on photosensitive stock, a process that was developed in a frenzy of scientific experimentation. The French inventor Nicéphore Niépce had some early success; his *View from the Window at Le Gras* (1827) is the oldest surviving photograph. After continued experimenting, the end of the century brought the development of photosensitive celluloid 'film', from which all photography derived until the digital age.

NICÉPHORE NIÉPCE

The first photograph (1827).

The Study of Motion

The English scientist Eadweard Muybridge used an impressive volley of cameras to establish whether horses lift all of their hooves from the ground mid-gallop (they do). His investigations improved camera shutter speed and led to faster emulsions.

EADWEARD
MUYBRIDGE

1. Camera in start position.

2. Shutter mechanically triggered by trip wire.

A horse galloping by a volley of cameras.

3. The shutter in closed finish position.

In 1879, Muybridge used his Zoopraxiscope invention to create the illusion of movement with captured sequential images. The device was elegant in its simplicity. Muybridge traced his photographs onto a glass disc, which was then spun in front of a light source to create an animated projection.

THE FIRST FILMMAKERS

The French engineer Louis Le Prince is the father of motion pictures. The earliest surviving film in existence is his *Roundhay Garden Scene* (1888), with a length of 2.11 seconds.

LOUIS LE PRINCE

Roundhay Garden Scene (1888)

Kodak film (1880s), similar to what Louis used.

60mm film spool for single-lens camera.

On his way to a promotional tour, Le Prince boarded a train in Dijon; but when it arrived in Paris, his awaiting friends found that he had disappeared. Le Prince was never seen again, prompting a mass of wild theories, including a murderous conspiracy engineered by rival inventor Thomas Edison.

Le Prince's Cameras

The *Roundhay Garden Scene* was shot using Le Prince's single-lens camera, which seems the most conventional to our modern minds. However, Le Prince also developed cameras with multiple lenses, including a sixteen-lens camera. Le Prince's cameras could be configured to each project; he referred to these modified devices as 'deliverers'.

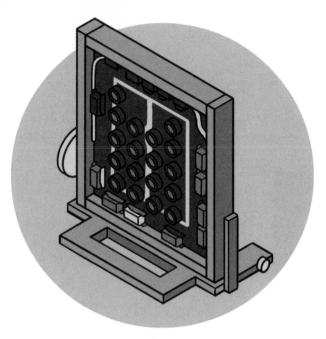

Sixteen-lens camera-projector (1886)

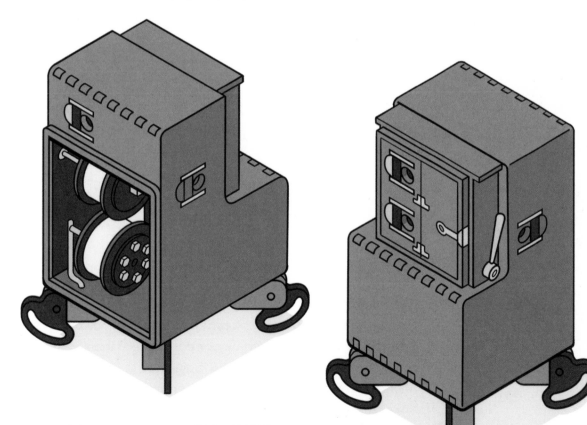

Single-lens camera-projector Mk2 (back) (1888)

Single-lens camera-projector Mk2 (front) (1888)

THE 1890s

In the 1890s, the public was enthralled with the unprecedented spectacle of motion pictures. For the first time, fleeting records of life could be repeatedly viewed and shared.

The Kiss (1896)

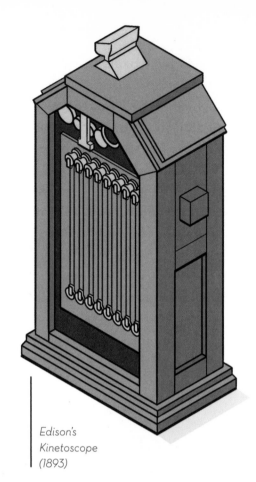

A chap enjoying 'The Kiss'.

Many were shocked by the raw obscenity, prompting condemnation by the Catholic church.

Edison's Kinetoscope (1893)

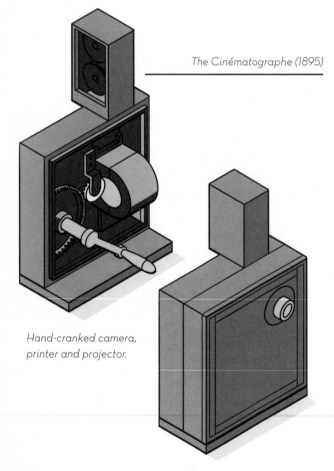
The Cinématographe (1895)

Hand-cranked camera, printer and projector.

Equipment Paradigms

Around this time, the infamously competitive inventor Thomas Edison introduced the Kinetoscope, inspired by Muybridge's Zoopraxiscope. The device permitted a viewer to look through a tiny peephole and see a moving image, which was created by a strip of film moving over a light source. Meanwhile, the French inventor Léon Bouly developed the Cinématographe (from which we take the word 'cinematography') and sold the patent to the Lumière brothers. The Cinématographe could be configured to capture footage and project images, allowing for public screenings.

The First Film Studios

Most early filmmakers relied on natural lighting. Edison's Black Maria, built in 1893, was the very first production studio and was reliant on sunlight. The studio stood on a rotating platform, which turned to let sunlight in for longer periods of time. A few years later, the German inventor Oskar Messter opened the first film studio in Berlin. Messter's experience in theater lighting gave him the foresight to install four Korting & Matthiessen 50-amp arc lamps, so filming was no longer limited to daylight hours.

THOMAS EDISON
(exhibiting his frown)

Retracting roof

A rotating platform for extending hours of direct sunlight.

The Black Maria (1893)

THE FIRST SCREENINGS

The Lumières were probably the first to publicly project films in as early as 1895 at Le Salon Indien du Grand Café in the center of Paris. The first time audiences saw *Arrival of a Train at La Ciotat Station* (1895), they were startled as the train seemingly thundered straight towards them. Strangely, the Lumières were not convinced of the potential of their machine, and would later abandon screenings in favor of other scientific enterprises.

The Cinématographe configured to project.

Le Salon Indien du Grand Café

Probably the first public film screening.

Mon Dieu!

AUGUSTE LUMIÈRE

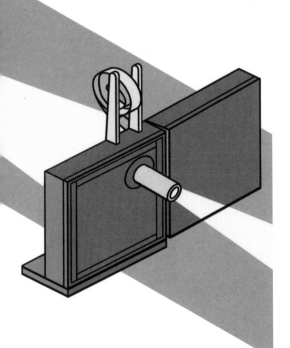

LOUIS LUMIÈRE

The Lumières' films were mostly candid depictions of everyday life, which they referred to as 'actualités'. They also made a handful of slapstick comedy films.

Arrival of a Train at Ciotat Station (1895)

The Sprinkler Sprinkled (1895)

Baby's Meal (1895)

20th CENTURY

THE 1900s

Motion pictures were sold worldwide, as were devices like the Kinetoscope and Cinématographe. As these motion pictures lacked sound, translation was not an issue.

Vaudevilles and Nickelodeons

Vaudeville houses were home to great variety shows, showcasing anyone from actors to acrobats. Judy Garland and Cary Grant would begin their careers as performers or 'vaudevillians' at these venues. Some vaudeville owners installed projection equipment, allowing short movies to be played as part of the program.

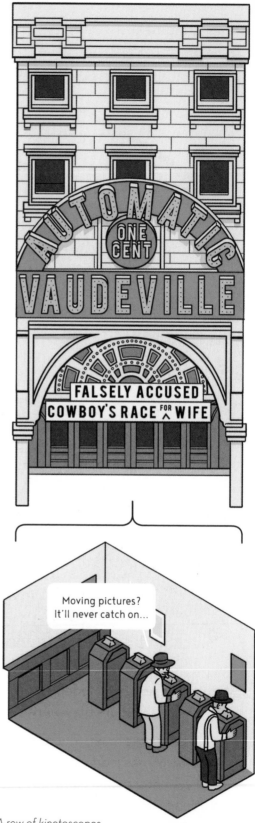

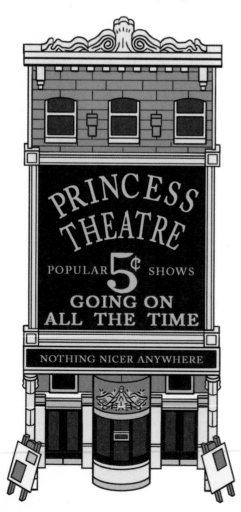

A row of kinetoscopes.

*A screening at a vaudeville.
Smoking was very common.*

Vaudevilles and nickelodeons were often frowned upon by high society types; in their twilight years they were seen as amoral and seedy.

The first purpose-built venues for viewing motion pictures were nickelodeons. The name comes from 'nickel', referring to the coin-operated machines inside (usually Kinetoscopes), and 'odeon', a modified Greek word meaning something like 'roofed theater'. The majority of early short movies exhibited were gags and soft pornography.

MAGIC AND ILLUSION

The Frenchman Georges Méliès was a versatile artist and magician who pioneered techniques such as the dissolve, superimposition, and time-lapse. His experience in set and costume design gave his films an imaginative style. His screenings were often part of a broader performance of magic tricks and mechanical puppetry.

GEORGES MÉLIÈS

JEHANNE D'ALCY

D'Alcy was one of the very first full-time actors.

During the First World War, the studio was appropriated as a hospital and film stock was recycled into shoe heels.

Méliès as Mephisto in
The Damnation of Faust (1818).

A gigantic puppet from
Conquest of the Pole (1912).

Big moon face in
A Trip to the Moon
(1902).

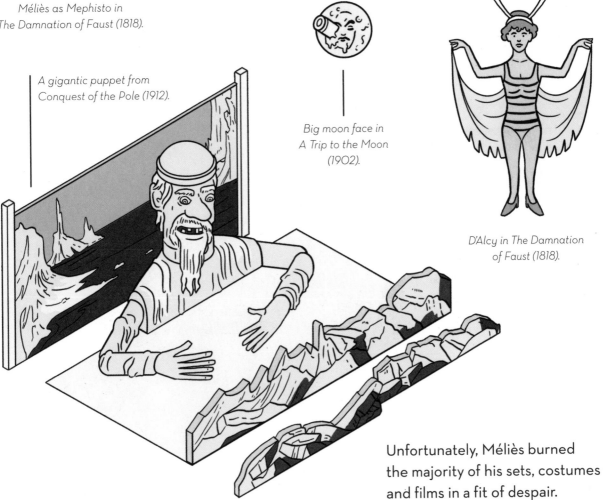

D'Alcy in The Damnation
of Faust (1818).

Unfortunately, Méliès burned the majority of his sets, costumes and films in a fit of despair.

THE 1910s

Thomas Edison co-founded the Motion Picture Patents Company (MPPC) in New Jersey, which enforced a ruthless patent monopoly. To avoid restrictive patent law, independents fled to California which offered natural splendor and excellent lighting conditions for filming. The most popular destination was a town called Hollywood, which would account for the majority of American production by 1915.

The Set of *Intolerance*

Spectacle

D.W. Griffith, an American director, was obsessed with spectacle and providing something new for audiences. Griffith was driven by nationalistic pride and racial hate, which was distasteful to the broader American audience even in the 1910s. His set pieces were gigantic and involved thousands of extras, but eventually his expenditure would sink his production company.

Intolerance (1916) was outrageously expensive to produce. The film flopped so badly that the associated studio had to be sold. The Babylon set stood derelict until 1919, when it was burned down. Griffith was financially ruined for the rest of his life.

Independent Productions

Oscar Micheaux was a wonderfully prolific African-American writer, producer and director. Micheaux held the passionate belief that one could achieve respect and success through hard work and enterprise; he had built a movie production company from scratch during a time when African-Americans were subjected to segregation and unmitigated prejudice. His movies were the antithesis of D.W. Griffith's work, and *Within Our Gates* (1920) in particular is seen as a direct response to the bigotry of Griffith's *Birth of a Nation* (1915).

OSCAR MICHEAUX

Micheaux actively advertised the banning of his movies to attract curious audiences.

Micheaux was known for personally promoting and distributing his movies to ensure African-American communities had a chance to see them.

EVELYN PREER

Pioneering actor.

Hyde Park Picture House opened in 1914, one of many movie theaters that screened news of the First World War.

Kaleen New Century Projector (1910), an early projection device used in movie theaters.

Popcorn carts commonly populated the streets. They were so popular that theaters began selling their own.

THE MOVIE THEATER

As resources were scarce during the First World War, many production teams focused on documenting the conflict. Purpose-built movie theaters were erected across Europe to broadcast newsreels and to provide an escape for audiences. Movie theaters had a much larger capacity than nickelodeons and were far more comfortable, so nickelodeons declined in popularity.

Ypres, Belgium, during the First World War (1914–1918).

Fearless Feats on Film

As the decade drew to a close, comic filmmakers such as Buster Keaton and Charlie Chaplin were incredibly popular. Comics were especially interested in the showmanship of film, employing stage magic and devious editing to excite and amuse audiences. The American camera operator Elgin Lessley was often the innovator behind the most spectacular camera tricks of the era, and his work with Keaton on *The Playhouse* (1921) involved nine Keatons appearing simultaneously.

BUSTER KEATON

One sequence filmed thrice

Custom aperture

Obscured footage

Masking allowed for multiple takes to be exposed onto one film strip. This is known as compositing.

The complete illusion from The Playhouse (1921).

MOVIE THEATERS THROUGH THE AGES

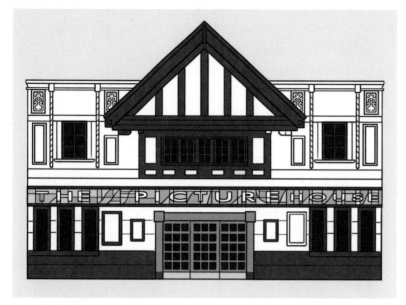

Stafford Picture House, Stafford, UK (1914)

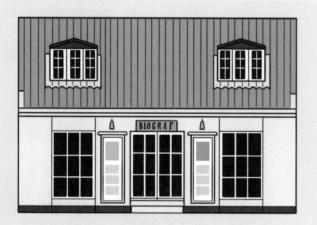

Dragør Biograf, Dragør, Denmark (1928)

Cine Thesion, Athens, Greece (1935)

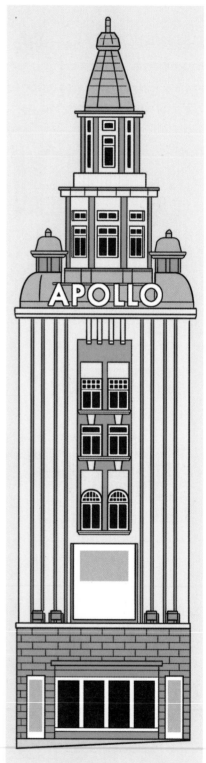

Apollo Kino, Vienna, Austria (1929)

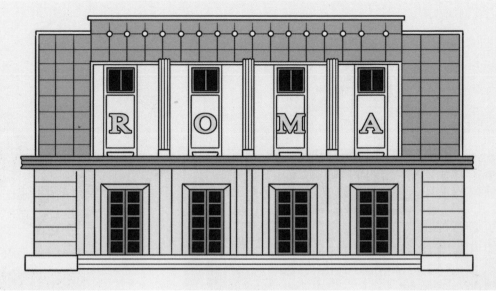

Cinema Roma, Asmara, Eritrea (1937)

4 Star Cinema, Kilgore, USA (1987)

Cinémathèque Leipzig, Leipzig, Germany (1991)

Norton Street Cinema, Sydney, Australia (1998)

THE 1920s

After the civil war in Russia, the newly formed Soviet Union faced the task of rejuvenating its film industry. The stand out pioneer in state-sponsored shorts was Dziga Vertov. Vertov and his team condensed profound social messages into short films using a technique called "montage", in which sequences of clips were edited together with bold titles.

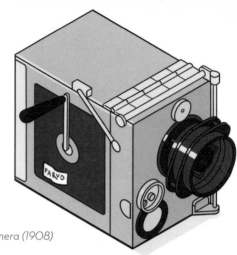

Parvo camera (1908)

Humorous montage, comparing hygienic routine with that of cleaning around the city.

DZIGA VERTOV

A stunt in Man With a Movie Camera (1919), in which the operator stood in front of a speeding train.

Fresh Filmmaking Communities

Weimar Germany was a melting pot of artistic movements such as Futurism and Cubism, with the Bauhaus school of art forging new paths in learning and artistic expression. This rousing environment nurtured the German expressionist film movement. The Austrian director Fritz Lang's *Metropolis* (1927) is a perfect example of this aesthetic, although Lang was reportedly rather harsh on his performers and crew.

FRITZ LANG

Brigitte Helm in costume.

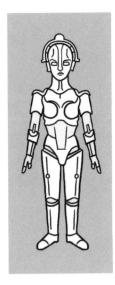

Brigitte Helm as the Maschinenmensch.

Lang subjected the cast of Metropolis to grueling conditions

SOUND!

Before sound movies or 'talkies', music was performed live alongside the projection of a movie. Orchestras would play arrangements for screenings at vaudevilles and spacious theaters, while pianists and mechanical musical devices accompanied the smaller nickelodeons. The grander movie palaces built in the 1920s often included large theater organs.

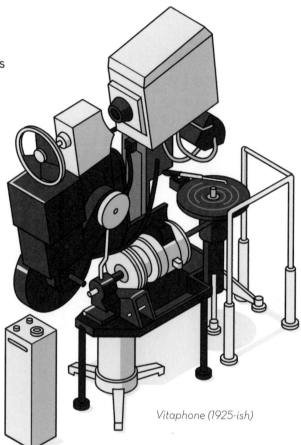

Vitaphone (1925-ish)

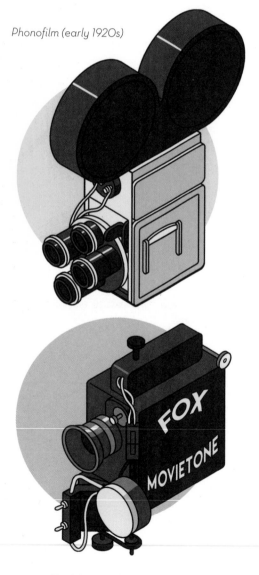

Phonofilm (early 1920s)

Fox Movietone camera (1926)

Early Sound Equipment

The Warner Brothers' Vitaphone was a disc format which gave *The Jazz Singer* (1927) its voice. Once the public had experienced film with sound, there was no return. The Vitaphone itself proved difficult to synchronize with footage, and was followed by a flurry of developments. The Phonofilm and Movietone would remove the difficulties of synchronization by including sound information directly on the filmstrip. By the end of the decade, synchronized sound was the standard for motion picture entertainment.

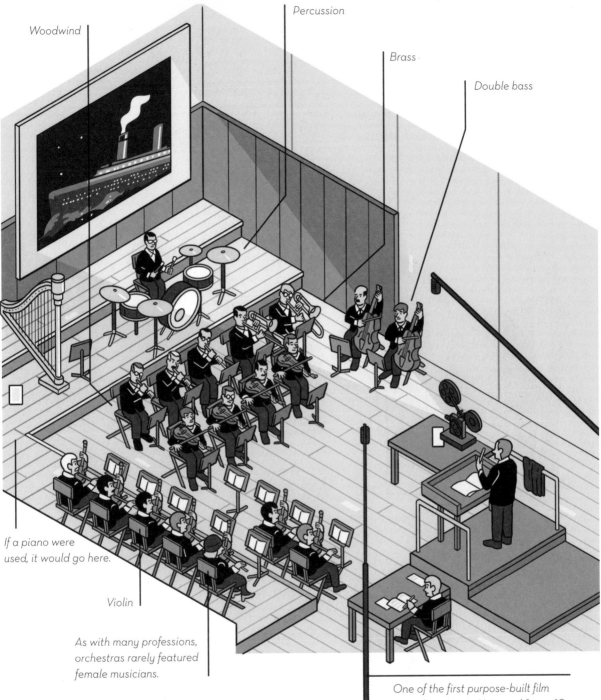

Woodwind

Percussion

Brass

Double bass

If a piano were used, it would go here.

Violin

As with many professions, orchestras rarely featured female musicians.

One of the first purpose-built film recording stages, Universal Stage 10.

Lost in Translation

When sound was introduced, audiences were divided by language. The musical genre initially bridged the gap, as dialogue took a back seat to the melody and dance routines. Some productions were filmed in multiple languages. The German director Ewald André Dupont's *Atlantic* (1929) was shot in both German and English by quickly switching out the main cast between takes.

THE 1930s

The Great Depression took a heavy toll on movie admissions. Exhibitors responded by offering more value for viewers' money with double features. These often included a more cheaply made 'B-feature', followed by the higher quality 'A-feature'.

Frankenstein (1931)

Bride of Frankenstein (1935)

Flash Gordon (1936)

The Invisible Man (1933)

Directors as Stars

Kenji Mizoguchi's movies responded to Japan's transition from feudalism to modernity. He is known for his use of extended shots, which required fastidious attention to sets and props from art director Hiroshi Mizutani. His meticulous approach to every aspect of production greatly influenced his contemporaries, and would inform the international New Wave in the 1960s.

Osaka Elegy (1936)

KENJI MIZOGUCHI

Mise en scène applied to direct the viewer's gaze and communicate tone.

ALFRED HITCHCOCK

The 39 Steps (1935)

The English director Alfred Hitchcock rose to high acclaim in the 1930s. He combined techniques of montage with the tension of German silent cinema to create a series of masterful thrillers. One technique he seemed eager to apply was rear projection. The method involves projecting footage behind filmed action. For example, *The 39 Steps* (1935) uses rear projection to create the illusion of movement outside train carriages.

COLOR!

Early attempts to add color to film involved tinting the stock, which interfered with the sound information exposed on its margins. The American Joseph A. Ball and his engineers built 3-strip Technicolor cameras that separated light using a prism. The spectrums of light were exposed onto 3 corresponding negatives. The developed stock was dyed and transferred onto another stock bearing the sound information.

Technicolor camera (1932)

Films sensitive to blue and red light are exposed.

Film sensitive to green light is exposed.

Light enters through the lens.

Magenta filter splits the light.

The exposed film is dyed in their color.

A single strip for the soundtrack is added.

The four strips are united through a mechanical printing process.

Three-strip Technicolor camera

Colorful Characters

For the first time, costume departments were liberated to explore the full spectrum of color and found new ways to convey narrative through costume.

udy Garland as Dorothy
The Wizard of Oz (1939).

Errol Flynn as Robin Hood in
The Adventures of Robin Hood (1938).

Frank Morgan as the gatekeeper
in The Wizard of Oz (1939).

A costume featured
in The Women (1939).

Gone with the Wind (1939) The first color movie to receive an Oscar.

You should be kissed and often, and by someone who knows how.

THE 1940s

During the Second World War, the Soviet Union sent at least 400 cameramen to the front line to capture footage. The Nazi party completely nationalized the German film industry, using it as a tool of social manipulation. It is estimated that over 45 million people attended Nazi film screenings.

Arriflex 35mm (1937)

Looks a little too similar to a gun, especially from a distance in a combat scenario.

Pistol-like grip. Held just like a submachine gun.

Khaki coloration.

Cunningham Combat Camera (1945)

Weapons of War

In 1937, the German company Arnold & Richter developed the first reflex 35mm motion picture camera called the Arriflex 35. It had an innovative reflex shutter which enabled the operator to view the image as it was being captured on film. One peculiar imitation was the American Cunningham Combat camera, which looked remarkably like a weapon because of its rifle-shaped profile and khaki finish.

Films from the Front Line

The Office of War Information recruited Hollywood directors and actors to produce propaganda. Frank Capra, known for *It's a Wonderful Life* (1946), directed the *Why We Fight* series including *Prelude to War* (1942). John Ford was drafted into service and produced military training videos such as *Sex Hygiene* (1941).

A Low Point in Humanity (1945)

Aircraft were fitted with film cameras for espionage and testing.

FILM NOIR

The film noir genre thrived on the tension and terror of the war. Film noir cinematography was heavily influenced by the German Expressionism of the 1920s, showing a similar obsession with capturing sharp forms through a mixture of lighting, set design and costume. The marvelous Orson Welles produced, directed and starred in his movie *Citizen Kane* (1941), which is perhaps the first of this genre. The non-linear story is relayed by a variety of biased narrators, creating a disjointed mystery for the viewer to solve.

ORSON WELLES

Director, actor and Martian invasion hoaxer.

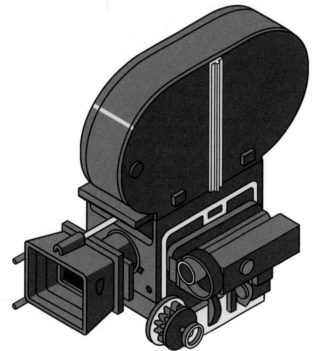

Mitchel BNC (1935)

You talk of the people as though you own them.

Citizen Kane (1941)

Welles's magnum opus, and probably the definitive film of its genre.

Young Kane

Old and cranky Kane

GREGG TOLAND

The American cinematographer Gregg Toland pioneered various techniques to capture striking deep focus footage. This meant that the foreground, middle-ground and background of a shot were all in focus, allowing scenes to be dense with action and subtle meaning. Toland modified a Mitchell BNC camera with a remote focus mechanism, and strategically placed carbon arc lamps to intensify the lighting conditions required for the deep focus effect.

THE 1950s

Movie attendance gradually fell during the 1950s. One contributing factor was the post-war exodus of young families from the theater-packed cities into quiet suburbs. Studios addressed this problem by building drive-in theaters which often showed double features to entice audiences with tight budgets.

Debbie Reynolds,
Singin' in the Rain (1950)

Destination Moon
(1950)

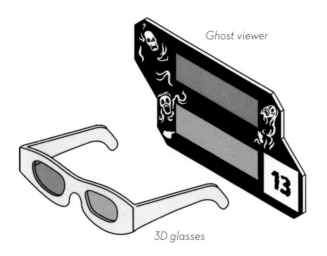

Ghost viewer

3D glasses

Gimmicks

Many movies and movie theaters experimented with gimmicks to attract audiences. William Castle was particularly known for his creative devices. During performances of *The Tingler* (1959), timed buzzers in seating gave audiences a jolt when the titular parasite appeared on screen.

Drive-in movie

Widescreen

The French astronomer and inventor Henri Chrétien developed an anamorphic lens for tanks during the First World War. His lenses were oval-shaped, allowing a 180-degree field of view, and were used to create the CinemaScope widescreen effect. The American camera technician Robert Gottschalk continued this work and built the Panavision camera, which would become standard equipment by the late 1960s.

Anamorphic lenses were developed for French tanks.

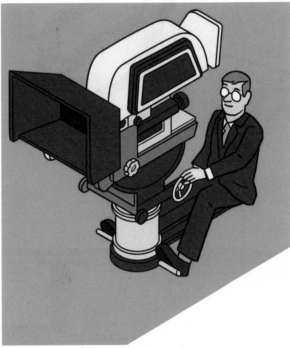

Early Panavision camera

Normal Lens

Anamorphic lens *Squeeze in that extra horizontal detail!*

SAMURAI AESTHETIC

After the war, the Japanese movie industry was liberated from Imperial nationalization. A new breed of ambitious directors emerged, the most influential of which was Akira Kurosawa. Kurosawa, like Mizoguchi before him, was a master of mise en scène; the composition of set pieces, props and actors were all highly considered to communicate narrative.

AKIRA KUROSAWA

Beautifully balanced mise en scène in Rashomon (1950).

There is nothing that says more about its creator than the work itself.

Kurosawa painted his very own concept art and storyboards.

Yojimbo (1961)

SANJURO

Seven Samurai (1954) resonated with international audiences and had a lasting impact on subsequent action movies. Kurosawa's later work *Yojimbo* (1961) was unofficially adapted by Sergio Leone in his Western *A Fistful of Dollars* (1964).

THE MAN WITH NO NAME

A Fistful of Dollars (1964)

The Set of *Seven Samurai*

Kurosawa had a fastidious attention to world-building, producing fictional biographies and extremely detailed reference books.

Working with the cinematographer Asakazu Nakai, Kurosawa organised three separate camera groups to work simultaneously in order to capture as much action as possible, even if candid!

Tally sheets were used to record the number of bandits 'killed' to ensure continuity.

Seven Samurai was the most expensive movie ever made in Japan. Budget issues caused the production to stop several times, but apparently Kurosawa was confident that the movie would be completed. He simply went fishing during breaks.

EDITING

Film editing is the practice of applying structure and a visual language to moving images. The very first films were pretty much moving vignettes, and lacked what we now expect in continuity.

Filmmakers became more ambitious towards the end of the 1890s and included multiple shots within one production. Prior to the invention of specialist equipment, the first editors used scissors and tape to literally cut and join copies of the negative.

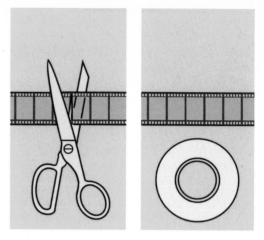

Scissors and tape; the original editing tools.

Early editing set up (1890s).

Moviola (1924)

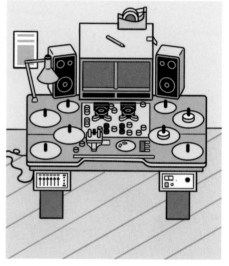

Steenbeck flatbed (patented 1934)

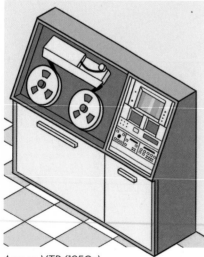

Ampex VTR (1950s)

Opportunities for Women

The creative industry had a tradition of prejudice towards women, something which has unfortunately endured. However, in the early days of moviemaking, editing was considered a technical role which allowed many women to enter the industry and have significant authorship in movies.

THELMA SCHOONMAKER

Martin Scorsese's film editor.

CMX editing suite (1970s)

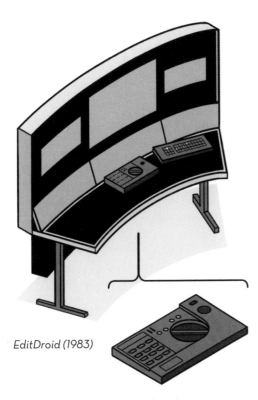

EditDroid (1983)

Modern-ish editing suite.

ANNE V.COATES

DEDE ALLEN

BEENA PAUL

THE 1960s

Hollywood's Production Codes, which set out the moral guidelines for all major studios, buckled under repeated offenses. America's filmmakers and audiences alike had long been exposed to liberal scenes of sex and violence thanks to European cinema. In addition, a post-Stalinist Russia was free to explore themes that had previously been forbidden by the regime.

GORDON PARKS

Civil Rights

The Civil Rights Movement in America encouraged filmmakers to address and explore complex racial issues. The photographer and filmmaker Gordon Parks became the first African-American to direct a movie with a major studio. His debut production *The Learning Tree* (1969) was an adaption of his partially autobiographical novel. Parks had an exceptional amount of creative control over the project: he wrote the screenplay, composed the music, directed and co-produced the movie.

The Learning Tree (1969)

New Epics

India declared itself a democratic republic in 1950. Government funding nurtured national productions, and Hindi cinema in particular was highly productive. *Mughal-e-Azam* (1960) took over a decade to produce and was incredibly expensive. The art director M. K. Syed oversaw the production of huge, extravagant set pieces, some of which took over a month to build. The battle sequence alone involved over 8,000 soldiers in full armor.

ASIF KARIM

Director of Mughal-e-Azam

Mughal-e-Azam (1960)

THE FRENCH NEW WAVE

Leading the charge in filmmaking was the French New Wave, which promoted the director as an auteur and broke away from old conventions. Jean-Luc Godard preferred to avoid formal scripts and enjoyed beginning a day's filming with just a handful of notes to help improvise camera work, script and direction. Many movies of the time were overly concerned with clear continuity, but New Wave experimented with jarring jump-cuts to save production costs and challenge the viewer.

AGNES VARDA

Director of Cleo from 5 to 7

JEAN-LUC GODARD

Director

Cleo from 5 to 7 (1962)

MARIE VAN BRITTAN BROWN

Inventor of the closed-circuit camera for the home (1966).

PIERRE ANGÉNIEUX

One of the inventors of the modern zoom lens.

A Bolex camera fitted with an Angénieux 12-120 (1963)

Jean-Paul Belmondo, Pierrot le Fou (1965)

Jean Seberg, Breathless (1960)

Nizo Super 8 (1965)

In 1963, French engineer Pierre Angénieux marketed a zoom lens that could move from 12mm to 120mm; a considerable improvement compared to previous lenses. The new zoom lenses became popular with home movie Super 8 cameras as well as for larger commercial movies.

THE 1970s

Many movie productions assimilated and regurgitated other cultures. A whole range of 'exploitation' movies were made, including blaxploitation movies, which were specifically targeted to an African-American audience. While initially very popular and still influential, many blaxploitation movies did little more than reinforce stereotypes.

Richard Roundtree,
Shaft (1971)

Pam Grier,
Coffy (1973)

Movie Poster Process

Production photographers

Illustrator

HARLEM GROOVE

A fictional movie poster.

Early digital printing

An imitation Panaglide as used in Halloween (1978).

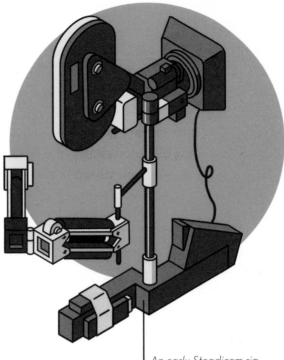

An early Steadicam rig used in Rocky (1976).

Magnificent Mobility

Historically, smooth movement was achieved with wheeled mounts called 'dollies'. Dollies relied on boards or tracks, which took time to assemble; and even the most careful operators could not eliminate shaky footage when carrying the camera. American camera operator Garret Brown invented the Steadicam in 1975. The Steadicam harness dampened the jolting movements of the operator, producing smooth footage at a lower cost than dolly systems. The system was imitated by various companies such as Panavision's Panaglide, but Steadicam has stood the test of time and continues to be used today.

Panavision camera

STAR WARS

The young George Lucas was already somewhat known for his movie *American Graffiti* (1973), when he approached 20th Century Fox with something he called *Adventures of Luke Starkiller, as taken from the Journal of the Whills, Saga I: The Star Wars*. He sacrificed $500,000 from his fee in order to take all merchandising and licensing fees, which would ultimately make him incredibly rich. The movie was eventually known as *Star Wars* (1977) and changed popular culture forever.

The movement of the camera around the stationary TIE fighter creates the illusion of flight.

GEORGE LUCAS

Director and writer

MARCIA LUCAS

Editor

PAUL HIRSCH

Editor

RICHARD CHEW

Editor

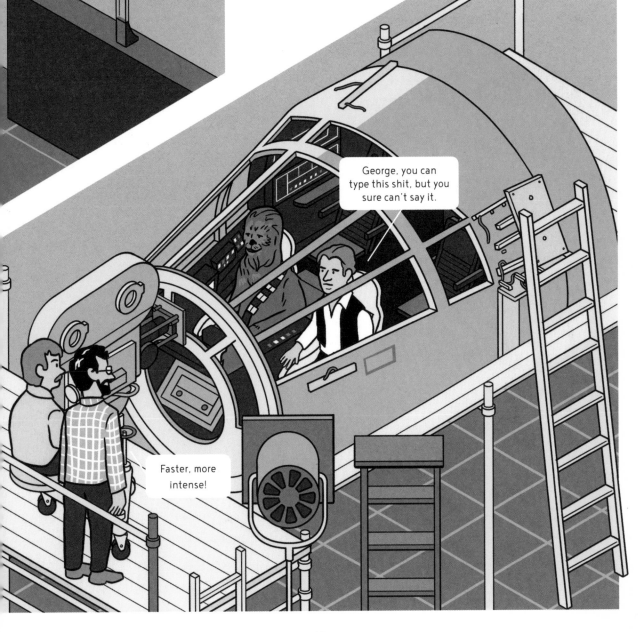

Originally, the TIE fighters had blue detailing, but it was removed to avoid issues with the chroma key (see page 87).

Revolutionary Visual Effects

The post-production of Star Wars involved a revolutionary combination of special effects. Everything from the use of miniatures, blue screen, costumes and symphonic score created a cinematic masterpiece that has enthralled audiences for over 40 years.

The Set of *Star Wars*

Apparently, the sandcrawler set was misinterpreted as a military vehicle by Libyan officials. To de-escalate tension, the Tunisian government asked Lucas to dismantle the set and move further away from the border.

'Jawas' were played by little people and children.

On set photographs reveal several interesting ways the crew tried to stay cool under the Tunisian sun.

This R2 unit has
a bad motivator!

Many of the original sets remain
to this day as relatively popular
tourist attractions.

The C-3PO costume didn't allow the actor,
Anthony Daniels, to sit down. A portable
board was built for him to lean on.

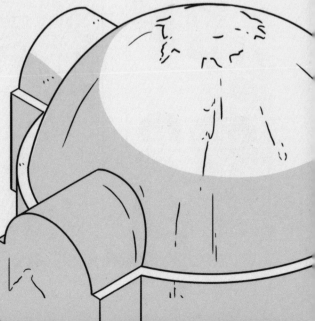

THE 1980s

The constant pursuit of the next biggest blockbuster led studios to spend more on each movie, meaning creative decisions were often based on what would generate profits. The wildly successful Star Wars franchise proved that returns from merchandising could far exceed those from the box office.

Betamax

The Betamax War

The VHS became triumphant in the format war with Betamax, leading to a boom in the VHS rental and sale market. The straight-to-video market allowed many filmmakers to distribute their movies at low cost.

VHS (Video Home System)

CGI

Computer-generated imagery, born in the 1960s, developed rapidly in the 1980s as the computer became more widely used in the workplace and at home. *Tron* (1982) featured an ambitious 15 minutes of 3D rendered imagery, while *Indiana Jones and the Last Crusade* (1989) involved the first digital composite to create a rapid aging effect without cutting away.

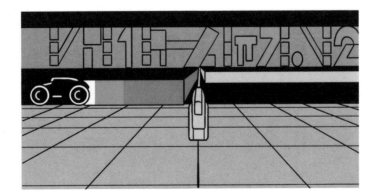

Tron CGI sequence

SYNTHETIC ENVIRONMENTS

The American director Stanley Kubrick was fastidious in his approach to pre-production. For *2001: A Space Odyssey* (1968), Kubrick collaborated with NASA and science fiction writer Arthur C. Clarke to create an accurate portrayal of futuristic space technology.

STANLEY KUBRICK

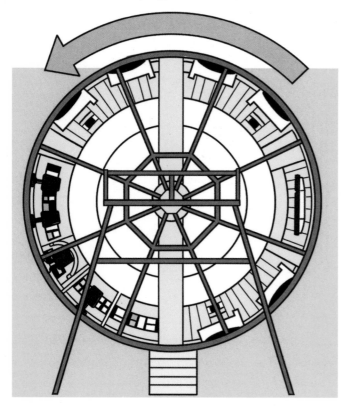

Illusion of centripetal space station achieved with a gigantic centrifuge.

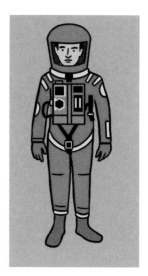

Keir Dullea as Dave in 2001: A Space Odyssey.

The camera was fixed inside the centrifuge, making it seem that Keir Dullea was the one in motion.

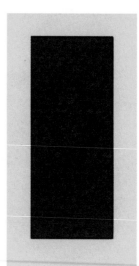

The Monolith.

His Vietnam war movie *Full Metal Jacket* (1987) was shot entirely in England, but Kubrick imported a small forest of palm trees from Spain to create the impression of a tropical location. Obsessive photographic research also helped set and costume designers to create an accurate façade of war-torn Vietnam during the 1960s and 70s.

The Vietnam set, built entirely on a London location.

THE 1990s

Elements from two competing disc formats were combined to create the Digital Versatile Disc (DVD). DVDs offered far more than VHS, as they had superior quality, more storage and were cheaper to manufacture. Broadcast television viewership continued to decline compared to cable networks. The TiVo digital video recorder debuted in 1999, starting the era of on-demand video.

Toshiba SD-2006 DVD player (1997)

A loose interpretation of a teenager's bedroom in the 1990s.

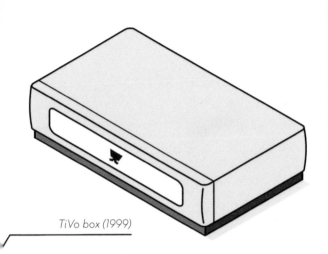

TiVo box (1999)

The Digital Age

Sony's Solid State Electronic Cinematography cameras were responsible for the first all-digital movie, *Rainbow* (1996). *Star Wars: Episode I – The Phantom Menace* became the first movie to be widely projected digitally using the prototype DLP cinema projectors, leading Lucas to film the subsequent *Star Wars* prequels entirely digitally.

Sony HDW-F900R (2000)

DVD keep case

Early digital projector

DIVERSE DISTRACTIONS

During the 1990s, the succession of increasingly impressive blockbusters escalated. Many movies in this period were characterized by dramatic explosions and over-the-top set-pieces. As this mania grew, so did ticket sales, and *Titanic* (1997) became the first movie to gross over a billion dollars. The price of movie admission tickets inflated and general attendance increased as multiplexes became the norm.

Big fiery explosions in movies are manufactured with lots of gasoline.

'Real' explosions are less cinematic, generally consisting of a brief flash followed by dust and smoke.

Speed (1994)

Sandra Bullock learned how to drive a bus just for her role!

Dreamy Direction

The American director, musician and actor David Lynch had a burst of productivity in the 1990s, with movies such as *Wild at Heart* (1990) and *Twin Peaks: Fire Walk With Me* (1992). Lynch takes inspiration from dream logic, and with every project his works seems to become increasingly peculiar. Movie critics often extract their own meaning from his movies, painting them as subversions of popular culture or as surrealist art.

Lynch prefers informal and conversational auditions.

It's better not to know so much about what things mean.

Protective socks to prevent tarnishing the floor polish.

The zigzag pattern previously appeared in Eraserhead (1977), adorning Alex's lobby.

21ˢᵗ CENTURY

THE 2000s

The emergence of the internet overwhelmed older media. Laptops, smartphones and tablets became more affordable and portable, allowing consumers to view content nearly anywhere. Services such as Netflix and Hulu further freed viewers from the constraints of the TV timetable. Peer-to-peer formats proved harmful to the movie and television industries, as some people found they could easily access content illegally on torrent and video streaming sites.

More affordable and user-friendly devices made piracy much more commonplace.

Peer-to-peer file sharing.

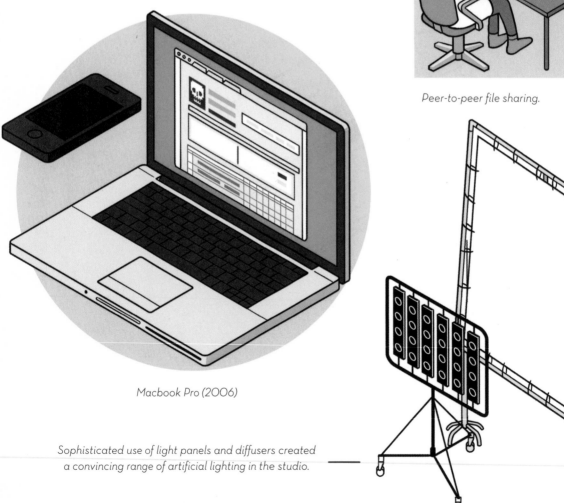

Macbook Pro (2006)

Sophisticated use of light panels and diffusers created a convincing range of artificial lighting in the studio.

Chroma Key

Chroma key is a post-production process that involves removing or replacing a specific range of color from footage. Typically, it is used to combine separate pieces of footage, creating the illusion that objects and actions occupy the same space. Technological advances in the 2000s made compositing the footage far easier. First-time director Kerry Conran's *Sky Captain and the World of Tomorrow* (2004) made extensive use of this technique, and was filmed almost entirely against green screen backdrops using a Sony HDW-F900. The filming itself took a measly 24 days, while the vast majority of time, effort and cost went into CGI effects created in post-production.

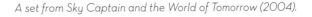

A set from Sky Captain and the World of Tomorrow (2004).

CULTURAL EXCHANGE

Hero (2002) was a triumph of cinematography, art, design and choreography from Chinese director Zhang Yimou and Australian-born cinematographer Christopher Doyle. During pre-production, locations were chosen to communicate emotions through colors and lighting; the script was re-written according to the feelings evoked by the climate. In one instance, filming had to be delayed until the leaves of a forest turned a specific hue of yellow.

Arriflex 535 (1990)

ZHANG YIMOU

CHRISTOPHER DOYLE

The related scene; a glorious celebration of color.

THE 2010s

Superhero, science fiction and fantasy movies became very popular during this decade. Marvel Studios devised a shared cinematic universe structure, allowing various characters and stories to exist both in their own movies and in productions that included ensemble casts. Other franchises would attempt to follow suit with varying degrees of success, such as *Star Wars* and the *Universal Monsters* movie series.

Both blue and green screens offer their own advantages. One advantage to the highly saturated green is its rarity in clothing.

A set piece from Avengers (2012), constructed from a mixture of practical props and use of green screen.

Marvelous Motion Capture

Motion capture dramatically improved with the introduction of computer-aided design. After his experience of portraying Gollum for *The Lord of the Rings* series, Andy Serkis co-founded The Imaginarium in 2010, a company specializing in motion capture-aided animation.

ANDY SERKIS

The contraption used to simulate the weightless movements in space.

The principle filming of the Mexican Alfonso Cuarón's *Gravity* (2013) involved a great deal of close-ups of the actors' faces. To help the actors respond to something more than a green screen, the production team built 'Sandy's cage'. The cage was walled entirely with responsive LEDs which conjured images for the actors to look at and lit their faces more accurately than a spotlight.

JUPITER?

The LED light box creating the 360 degree imagery of high orbit.

Custom Bot & Dolly Iris robotic camera rig (2013)

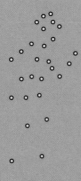

The actor's movements are tracked using a special body suit.

Vast teams of animators work extremely hard to translate and improve the raw movement data.

Eventually, fully computer-generated characters may be added in place of live action.

SYNTHESIS

During the 2000s, big-budget blockbusters involved more and more computer generated environments, effects and characters, an approach that began to wear on critics and audiences.

Immortan Joe!

Valhalla!

GEORGE MILLER

MARGARET SIXEL

Editor

Other filmmakers returned to practical effects with CGI for enhancement, rather than relying solely upon it. *Mad Max: Fury Road* (2015), directed by the Australian George Miller, made extensive use of spectacular stunt work, pyrotechnics and on-location filming to create a visceral, standout action movie.

JENNY BEAVAN

Costume designer

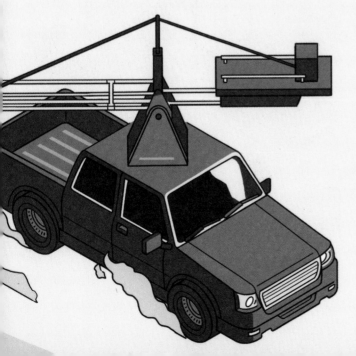

Hugh Keays-Byrne as Immortan Joe

Charlize Theron as Furiosa

THE FUTURE

With this sort of book, it is customary for the author to make a silly prediction about the future. I most definitely look forward to reviewing this portion of the book in a couple of decades from the comfort of my hover-chair.

A virtual reality headset. (2018)

Augmented reality 'Snap Spectacles', a precursor to a future of omnipresent filming? (2016)

VR or AR devices will likely become as commonplace as smartphones are today.

Holographic projection or AR could supersede the classic home fixture of the TV set.

New Realities

So, what's at the forefront of technology right now? Video games frequently outperform movies, which I would say is a case for audiences wanting more interactive experiences. Recently, Gareth Edwards, the director *of Rogue One: A Star Wars Story* (2016) used a virtual reality (VR) headset in order to direct footage that was completely computer-generated.

The handset acts as an interactive window into pre-rendered footage.

The director 'films' virtual pre-rendered action using the handset.

A vast team of animators polish the animation based on the director's input.

Augmented reality handset (several devices strapped together).

Augmented reality has existed for a good while, but it will take a few years for it to become a truly seamless experience. Perhaps decades from now, glasses or contact lenses will be able to augment the viewer's environment into a cinematic experience.

HERITAGE

As movie attendance continues to slide, some exhibitors have offered interactive screenings such as those arranged by Secret Cinema in London. Audiences arrive dressed according to the aesthetic of the movie and are entertained by the screening as well as by a host of actors, set pieces and other interactive elements. This experience is remarkably similar to that of vaudeville houses. Many of the very first movie theaters from the 1910s are still in operation and have become much-loved heritage centers for communities, often showing a range of classic and cult films.

A thrilling scene in Back to the Future (1985), projected and recreated for a live audience simultaneously.

A 'Secret Cinema' screening: a fantastic gimmick or a return to vaudeville?

Small productions streamlined by accessible tech.

Easier distribution via streaming services.

Solitary kinetoscope.

Theater crowd experience.

Shared home media.

Solitary VR experience.

The context in which we view film will change. The intimacy of Edison's Kinetoscope was replaced by the shared experience of the movie theater, while today the appealing comfort and convenience of home media has reduced theater attendance. One constant in the chaotic journey of filmmaking is the pioneering spirit of technological investigation; we will always explore new ways to share our stories.

MEET THE TEAM

DIRECTION

Director

Overseer of the creative aspects of filmmaking. A director influences nearly all aspects of production, including how an actor performs and technical aspects such as how scenes are shot.

Second Unit Director

Overseer of secondary footage, for example insert shots and special stunt sequences.

Writer

The person responsible for writing the script.

PRODUCTION

Producer

Responsible for funding the movie, hiring crew members and is sometimes involved in creative decisions with the director.

Line Producer

A liaison between producers, studios and other departments; the line producer also has a main role in managing budget.

Production Manager

Supervises the logistics of filmmaking, which may include budget and timekeeping.

Unit Publicist

Liaises between the production team and the press.

LOCATIONS

Location Manager

Oversees how locations are used.

Location Scout

Responsible for researching and locating places to film.

CASTING

Casting Director

Chooses actors suitable to play in the movie.

CAMERAS, LIGHTING AND OTHER RIGGING

Director of Photography / Cinematographer

Chief of camera crew. Works with the director to decide on the use of cameras, stock and how shots are composed.

Camera Operator

A person who handles the camera on set.

Boom Operator

A person who handles microphones on set. Microphones are often attached to a telescoping pole, known as a 'boom pole'.

Gaffer

The head electrician in movie production.

Key Grip

Supervisor of all rigging, lighting, camera movement and camera cranes. Works closely with the director of photography.

Best Boy/Girl

An assistant to the gaffer and key grip.

PRODUCTION DESIGN / ART DEPARTMENT

Production Designer

Responsible for the aesthetics of a movie, including the sets and costumes.

Art Director

Reports to the production designer. Has a more hands-on approach to working with artists to make the creative vision possible.

Set Designer

A draftsman who designs practical sets for use in the movie.

Set Decorator

Responsible for furnishing and other props used on sets.

Set Dresser

A person who installs and removes furnishings and props.

Greensman

A person who installs both natural and artificial plants for sets and landscapes.

Illustrator

Draws representations of how things could look.

Graphic Designer

Responsible for the graphic elements used in the movie, including type, image and some props.

Construction Coordinator

Responsible for the building of sets.

Head Carpenter

Leads a group of carpenters and builders who create furniture and furnishings.

Prop Maker

Creates unique props that are used in the movie.

Key Scenic

Leads a group responsible for treating the set, for example making the environment seem older by artificially ageing it.

Weapons Master

Manages the use of guns, blades and other combat tools.

COSTUMES, HAIR AND MAKE-UP

Costume Designer
Responsible for the clothes actors wear.

Key Make-Up Artist
Head of the make-up department, plans and designs the make-up worn by actors, including prosthetics.

Key Hair
Head of the hairdressing department, in charge of styling the hair of actors.

SPECIAL EFFECTS

Special Effects Supervisor
Responsible for practical effects on set, such as explosions.

Stunt Coordinator
In charge of the stunt work on set.

Stuntman / Stuntwoman
Performs dangerous and highly skilled feats.

POST PRODUCTION

Film Editor
Assembles the shots to create the movie, works closely with the director.

Negative Cutter
Cuts and splices film negative before it is exposed in the lab.

Colorist
Manipulates the coloration of films by chemical or digital means.

Visual Effects Producer
Leads a department to break down a script into storyboards and figure out what requires visual effects such as miniatures or CGI.

Visual Effects Director
Responsible for the visual effects aesthetics of a movie, including CGI.

Rotoscope Artist
Manually remove or add effects. They may be used to hide stunt wires and rigging.

Matte Painter
Creates paintings to extend or modify an image.

SOUND

Sound Designer
In charge of how sound is applied to a movie.

Sound Editor
Applies sound to footage.

Re-recording Mixer
Balances the different sounds together.

Composer
Writes the musical score to a movie.
Sometimes leads the orchestra during
recording sessions as a conductor.

Foley Artist
Creates sound effects along to footage.
This often includes footsteps and the
sound of objects being handled.

ACTORS

Actor / Actress
A person who performs in a movie.

Extra
An actor who plays a minor role,
often in the background.

GLOSSARY

Anamorphic Lens
A lens that compresses a wider field of view into a narrower image, so circles appear to be oval. Requires another lens to 'desqueeze' the image.

Blimp
A housing built around old cameras to reduce the amount of noise they made.

Cut
A change in the camera position or angle.

Dolly
A small trolley usually fixed to tracks, allowing large cameras to move smoothly.

Film (verb)
To record a scene.

Film (noun)
A strip of material coated in light-sensitive emulsion, used to create sequential images.

Also a common synonym for motion picture.

Frame
A single image, part of a sequence of motion pictures.

Montage
Rapid cutting of footage to convey narrative or emotion.

Motion Picture
The broadest term applied to imagery that moves, including movies and animation.

Shot/s
A portion of motion footage.

Stock
The format of the film used to record scenes, for example 35mm or 70mm.

Mise en Scène
The aesthetic consideration of everything on a set.

Titles
Words that appear on screen.

Baudrillard, J., *Simulacra and Simulation* (Michigan, 2010 [1981])

Barnwell, J., *The Fundamentals of Film-Making* (Switzerland, 2008)

Benjamin, W., *The Work of Art in the Age of Mechanical Reproduction* (London, 2008 [1936])

Chopra-Gant, M., *Cinema and History: The Telling of Stories* (London, 2008)

Cousins, M., *The Story of Film* (London, 2004)

Dancyger, K., *The Technique of Film and Video Editing* (Oxford, 1997)

Draven, D., *Genre Filmmaking: A Visual Guide to Shots and Style* (Burlington, 2013)

Enticknap, L., *Moving Image Technology: From Zoetrope to Digital* (New York, 2005)

Fischer, L. (ed.), *Art Direction and Production Design: A Modern History of Filmmaking* (London, 2015)

Hurd, M., *Women Directors and Their Films* (Westport, 2006)

Keating, P. (ed.), *Cinematography: A Modern History of Filmmaking* (New York, 2015)

Nowell-Smith, G. (ed.), *The Oxford History of World Cinema* (New York, 1997)

Roberts, G., *Forward Soviet!: History and Non-fiction Film in the USSR* (New York, 1999)

Stokes, M. & Maltby, R. (eds.), *Hollywood Abroad: Audiences and Cultural Exchange* (London, 2004)

REFERENCES

INDEX

LOUIS
LE PRINCE

ROSCOE
ARBUCKLE

OSCAR
MICHEAUX

JIMMY
STEWART

CARY
GRANT

JEHANNE
D'ALCY

AKIRA
KUROSAWA

GEORGE
MÉLIÈS

THOMAS
EDISON

NINA MAE
MCKINNEY

LENI
RIEFENSTAHL

TOSHIRO
MIFUNE

JAMES
MASON

LOIS
WEBER

SURAIYA
JAMAAL
SHEIKH

INGRID
BERGMAN

STANLEY
KUBRICK

BUSTER
KEATON

ALICE GUY-
BLANCHÉ

GRETA
GARBO

MARILYN
MONROE

LOUIS
LUMIÈRE

AUGUSTE
LUMIÈRE

TALLULAH
BANKHEAD

FRITZ
LANG

CHARLIE
CHAPLIN

ORSON
WELLES

JOHN
ALCOTT

KENJI
MIZOGUCHI

DZIGA
VERTOV

SERGEI
EISENSTEIN

SEAN
CONNERY